Writing Builders

Frank and Fiona Build a
FICTIONAL STORY

by Rachel Lynette
illustrated by Jan Lieffering

Content Consultant
Jan Lacina, Ph.D.
College of Education
Texas Christian University

NORWOOD HOUSE PRESS
CHICAGO, ILLINOIS

Norwood House Press
P.O Box 316598
Chicago, Illinois 60631
For information regarding Norwood House Press, please visit our website at:
www.norwoodhousepress.com or call 866-565-2900

Editor: Melissa York
Designer: Craig Hinton
Project Management: Red Line Editorial

This book was manufactured as a paperback edition. If you are purchasing this book as a rebound hardcover or without any cover, the publisher and any licensor's rights are being violated.

Paperback ISBN: 978-1-60357-561-4

The Library of Congress has cataloged the original hardcover edition with the following call number: 2013010274

©2014 by Norwood House Press.
All rights reserved.
No part of this book may be reproduced without written permission from the publisher.
Manufactured in the United States of America in North Mankato, Minnesota.
233N—072013

Words in **black bold** are defined in the glossary.

My First Fictional Story

Have you ever entered a contest? Once I won a contest by guessing how many jelly beans were in a jar. A couple of weeks ago, I entered a different kind of contest. The contest was for writing **fictional** stories. I almost didn't enter at all because I didn't think I could write a good story. I had written stories about things that have happened to me in real life for school, but I wasn't sure if I could write one from my imagination.

Luckily, I have a really good friend named Fiona. She knows a lot about writing and gave me some good tips! I was really proud of my story. I was even more proud when I found out I had won second prize in the contest! I got a big red ribbon and I got to read my story out loud at a special ceremony. Maybe I will be an author when I grow up.

By Frank, age 9

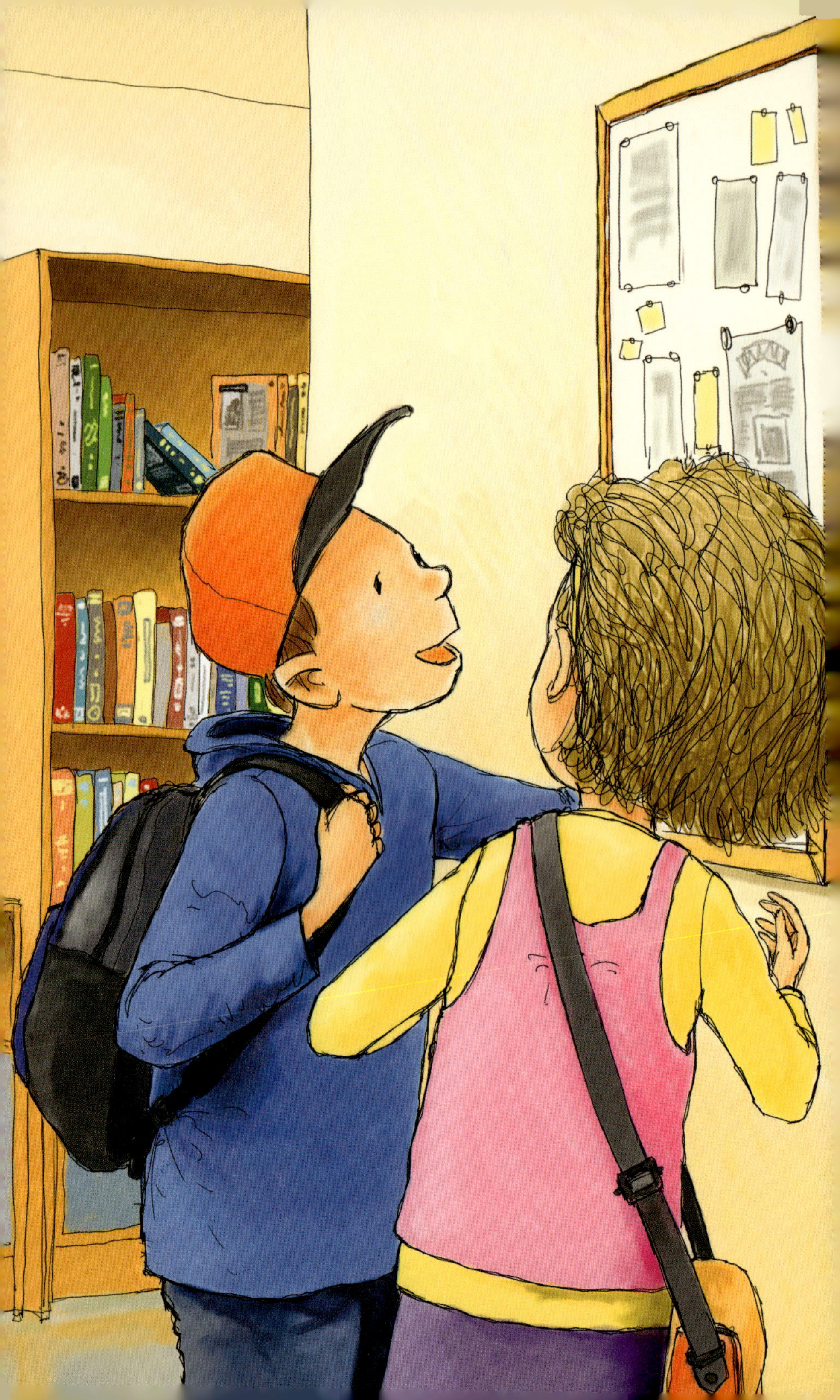

"Fiona, look at this," called Frank.

Fiona looked up from the book she was reading to see her friend Frank pointing to a poster on the library bulletin board. The poster was about a short-story contest the library was sponsoring.

"That sounds like fun," Fiona said. "Are you thinking of entering?"

"Well, I'd like to. Last week when I was playing with our class hamster, I got a really good idea for a story, but when I tried to write it, I got stuck after just a few sentences," Frank replied glumly.

"I think you should try it! My teacher says that some of the best ideas for fictional stories come from the author's real life," Fiona said enthusiastically. "Let's get the entry form from the librarian."

Fiona and Frank made their way to the check out desk and asked the librarian, Mrs. Jenkins, for an entry form. "I'm so pleased you are entering! Here is an entry form and a **story map**. Your story will come out much better if you organize your ideas before you begin writing."

Fiona leaned over Frank's shoulder to take a look. "I used a story map in school. Look, there's a place for each part of your story. You use this to plan and organize, right, Mrs. Jenkins?"

"You've got it!" replied Mrs. Jenkins. "I'll be over here if you have any questions."

Fiona and Frank went back to their table. Frank got right to work while Fiona went back to her book. "What do you think?" he asked Fiona when he was done.

entry form

STORY MAP

SETTING:
Classroom at first, then Alex's house

CHARACTERS:
- Alex—nine years old, loves animals and wants a pet of his own
- Alex's parents
- Alex's teacher, Mrs. Carson
- Nibbles the hamster

BEGINNING:
Alex's teacher lets him take the class hamster home for Christmas break.

MIDDLE:
The hamster gets out of his cage during the big Christmas party. Alex is able to find him before anything bad happens.

END:
Parents give Alex a puppy for Christmas because he took such good care of the hamster.

"That looks great!" Fiona said. "I can see that your story has a clear beginning, middle, and end. That is really important. I think you're ready to start writing." Frank got out some notebook paper and wrote:

> Once there was a boy named Alex. He was nine years old. He loved animals and he really wanted a pet of his own, but his parents wouldn't let him have one. Then his teacher asked him if he wanted to take the class hamster home for Christmas break.

He showed what he had written to Fiona. "Well, you've introduced the **main character**, which you should definitely do in the first part of a story, but I think you can do better," she said.

"Your story will be more interesting if you give your readers an idea of what your character is like rather than just telling them."

Frank looked confused. "I think I might have something that will help," said Fiona. "Hold on a second." Fiona dug around in her backpack and pulled out a notebook.

She added, "It's also good to make sure your readers know where the story is taking place. See, on your story map it says that the first **setting** is a classroom, but that isn't clear in what you wrote."

She handed Frank her notebook. "This is a story I'm working on for school. Just read the first part."

> Kasey wrinkled her nose as she opened the door to the chicken coop. It always smelled horrible. Carefully, she took the eggs from the nests and placed them in her big basket. As she worked, she thought about her old house in the city. She missed her friends. She wanted so much to be back in her fifth-grade classroom. Instead, she was stuck in the middle of nowhere doing farm chores and being homeschooled.

11

12

"Wow, that seems like a great story start," said Frank.

Fiona smiled. "I'm glad you like it! But you wouldn't have been as interested if I had just written, 'Kasey's family moved to a farm. Kasey did not like doing farm chores and being homeschooled. She missed her old house and friends in the city.'"

"It's better to have Kasey in the chicken coop since the story is about moving to a farm," Frank said. "I can picture it in my head that way. I also like knowing what she is thinking. It makes her seem more like a real person."

"Exactly," agreed Fiona. "You want to make your story as interesting as you can."

"And I want to make sure that the reader knows where the story is taking place," Frank said. "I think I have an idea."

Frank worked for a while longer and then showed his **revised** beginning to Fiona and Mrs. Jenkins:

"Thanks for cleaning the hamster cage again, Alex," said Mrs. Carson.

"Sure," said Alex. He put Nibbles gently onto the fresh bedding. "I like taking care of Nibbles. My parents won't let me have a pet. They say a pet is too much work for a nine-year-old."

"Well, you certainly take good care of Nibbles here at school," Mrs. Carson said.

"Much better," said Fiona. "I like how you used the word *gently* because it shows that Alex knows how to treat animals. I also think you did a good job using **dialogue** to let the reader know that Alex really wants a pet but can't have one."

"Dialogue is when you use quotation marks to show what your characters are saying, right?" asked Frank. "We've been working on that in school."

"Right! In a story, dialogue is a good way to show how a character reacts when something happens," explained Fiona. "In your dialogue, you showed that Alex is excited about getting to take care of Nibbles."

Frank worked on his story at home that evening and then again after school at the library the next day. He knew that Fiona would be there after her choir practice and he wanted to have something to show her. Things were going well until he got to the part about the big Christmas party. Frank stared miserably at his paper.

"Having trouble?" someone asked.

Frank turned to see Mrs. Jenkins standing behind him. "I sure am. I don't feel like I am describing the party well at all. This is what I wrote."

> Everything was fine until the night of his parents' big Christmas party. There were lots of people at the party. It was noisy and crowded.

"I see what you mean," said Mrs. Jenkins. "I think what you need are some **sensory details**. That will make the party come alive for your readers."

17

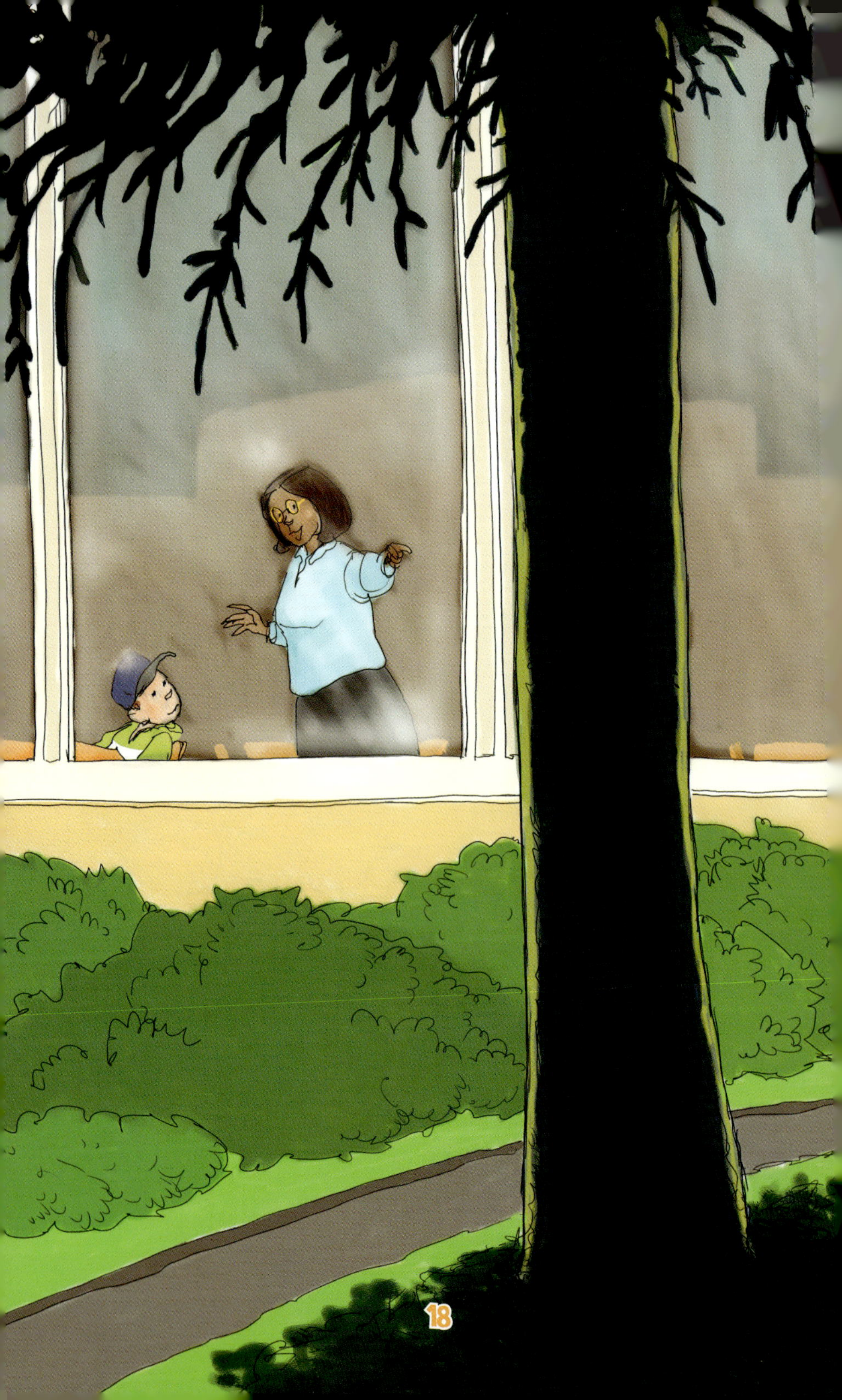

"Sensory details," said Frank thoughtfully. "That sounds familiar. Doesn't sensory have to do with your five senses?"

"Exactly. Describing something in a story goes beyond what you see with your eyes. Do you see that big pine tree by the parking lot? If you were out there now, what might you hear?" asked Mrs. Jenkins.

"Well, I might hear the wind blowing and maybe some birds chirping," said Alex.

"What would the tree feel like if you touched it?" prompted Mrs. Jenkins.

"The trunk would be rough and the needles would be sharp. I get it now. If I were out there, I would probably smell the pine needles. But what about taste? I'm not going to eat a pine tree!"

Mrs. Jenkins laughed. "Good point. You don't need to use all five senses for everything you describe, but adding one or two can make a big difference. Why don't you try it with your Christmas party?"

Frank got right to work. By the time Fiona arrived, he was ready to show her what he'd written.

Everything was fine until the night of his parents' Christmas party. The house was full of people. Everyone was talking and laughing. Grandpa was playing Christmas carols on the piano. The whole house smelled like gingerbread.

Later, Alex went to check on Nibbles. He knew something was wrong when he saw that his bedroom door was wide open. Then he saw that the door to Nibbles' cage was open too! First, he searched the cage. Next, he searched his room, but Nibbles was nowhere to be found!

"Great description," said Fiona. "You did a nice job with your **transitions**."

"I did?" asked Frank.

"Yes!" said Fiona. "Transitions help to move the story from one **event** to another without sounding choppy. Transitions are words and phrases like *first, after, then, next,* and *finally.*"

Frank wanted to keep working on his story, but it was time for him to meet his mom outside the library. He smiled to himself when he really did hear birds chirping. After dinner, Frank decided to skip watching television to work on his story instead. By bedtime, he had finished it!

The next morning, Frank read the ending he had written the night before. He had written:

After all the Christmas presents were opened, Alex's dad said that there was one more special present left, but he would have to get it. A few minutes later, he came through the door carrying the cutest puppy Alex had ever seen! "Merry Christmas," said Alex's dad as he gave the puppy to Alex. At last, Alex had a pet of his very own.

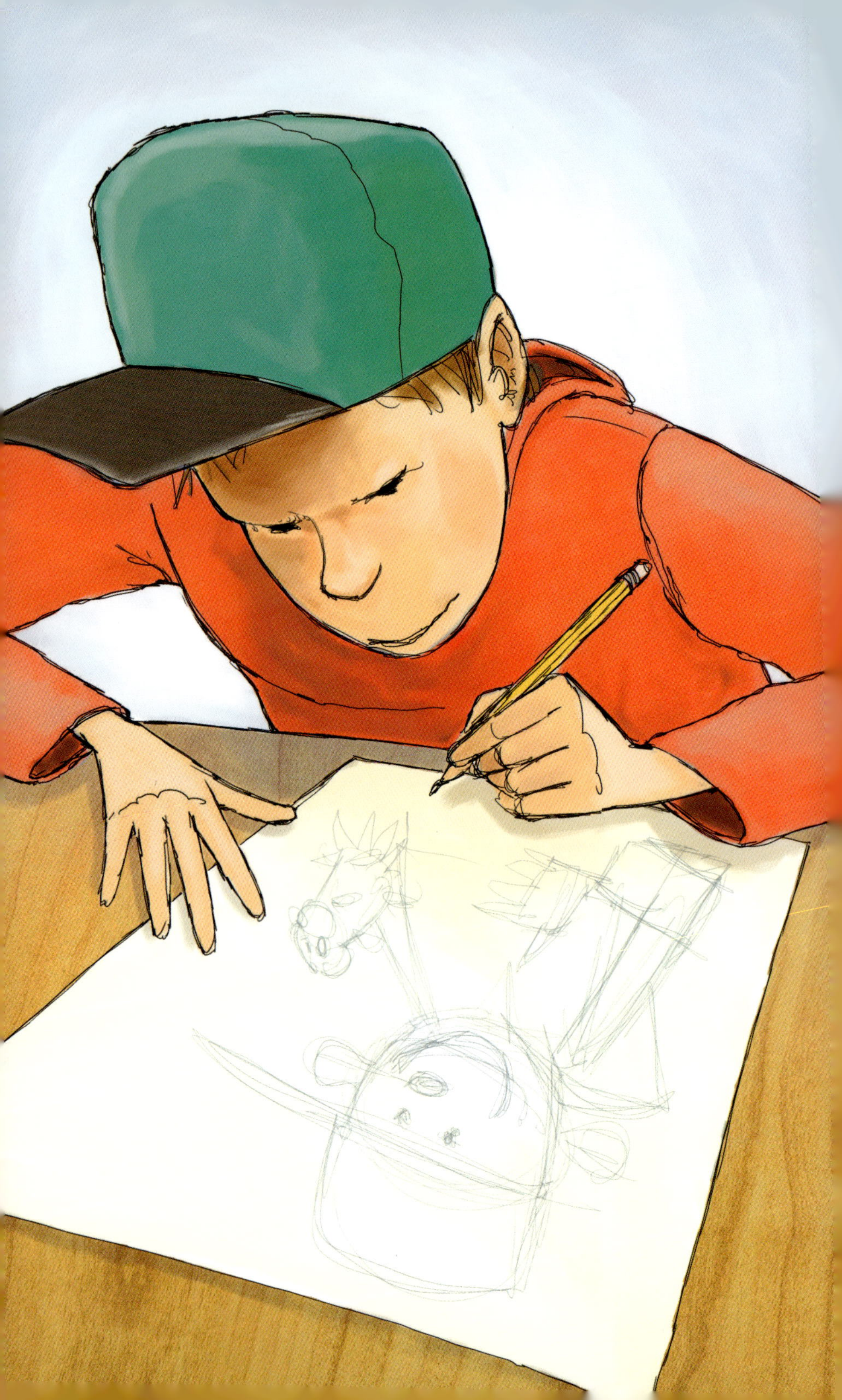

Frank reread the rest of his story. The problem was that the story was about taking care of Nibbles, but the ending didn't have anything to do with Nibbles. He needed to show how taking care of Nibbles was related to getting the puppy. Frank fixed the problem by changing what Alex's father said when he gave Frank the puppy:

"You took such good care of Nibbles that Mom and I realized you are ready to take care of a pet after all," Alex's dad said as he gave the puppy to Alex. At last, Alex had a pet of his very own.

Frank couldn't wait to show his story to Fiona. He didn't know if it was good enough to win the contest, but he was proud of it anyway. When he got to the library, he decided it would be nice to have an illustration to go with his story. He got a piece of blank paper from Mrs. Jenkins and drew a picture of Alex with Nibbles.

"Nice picture," said Fiona when she arrived. "Does this mean your story is done?"

"Yes," Frank said proudly, "and I couldn't have done it without your help."

HAMSTER ADVENTURE
by Frank

"Thanks for cleaning the hamster cage again, Alex," said Mrs. Carson.

"Sure," said Alex. He put Nibbles gently onto the fresh bedding. "I like taking care of Nibbles. My parents won't let me have a pet. They say a pet is too much work for a nine-year-old."

"Well, you certainly take good care of Nibbles here at school," Mrs. Carson said. "Do you think your parents would let you take care of him over Christmas break? It's only two weeks."

"That would be so great! I'll ask them tonight."

Alex was so excited about taking care of the hamster that his parents couldn't bear to tell him no. Taking care of Nibbles was fun. Alex made sure Nibbles had enough food and water. He played with him every day and always shut the cage door.

27

28

Everything was fine until the night of his parents' Christmas party. The house was full of people. Everyone was talking and laughing. Grandpa was playing Christmas carols on the piano. The whole house smelled like gingerbread.

Later, Alex went to check on Nibbles. He knew something was wrong when he saw that his bedroom door was wide open. Then he saw that the door to Nibbles' cage was open too! First, he searched the cage. Next, he searched his room, but Nibbles was nowhere to be found!

Alex started to panic. What if Nibbles got stepped on? Then he remembered that Nibbles liked dark, warm places. He went into the hall and saw the linen closet door was open. When he peeked inside, there was Nibbles, curled up between two pillows. "There you are! You really gave me a scare," he told the hamster.

The next day was Christmas. After all the Christmas presents were opened, Alex's dad said he had to get one more present. A few minutes later, he came through the door carrying the cutest puppy Alex had ever seen!

"You took such good care of Nibbles that Mom and I realized you are ready to take care of a pet after all," said Alex's dad. At last, Alex had a pet of his very own.

You Can Write a Fictional Story, Too!

You don't have to enter a contest to write a fictional story. Many people write stories for fun. You may even want to keep a list of story ideas so that you will always have something to write about. The following steps will help you:

Step 1: All stories start with an idea. Don't worry if you don't know everything that's going to happen right now—you can fill in the details as you plan and write your story.

Step 2: A story map can help you plan your story. You can use boxes to make a story map or make a list like the one Frank used. And you can always change your story later. A story map will help you think about your story's setting, characters, and plot. You can talk through your story map with a friend too!

Step 3: Start writing. Here are some tips to keep in mind:

- Make sure you introduce your main character and the setting in the beginning of your story.

- Keep your story interesting with sensory details.

- You can use dialogue to give the reader more information and to show how your characters react to things that happen in the story.

- Transition words will keep your story moving from one event to the next.

Step 4: Finally, write an ending that makes sense with the rest of the story.

Step 5: Revise. Read over your story and get a friend to read it too. Does the plot make sense? Can you add more vivid details?

Step 6: Write your final draft on clean paper or on a computer. Then share your story with your friends and family!

Here is something fun to try. Find an interesting picture in a magazine. Use the picture as a story prompt. A prompt is anything that gives you an idea for writing. You don't have to write about exactly what you see. Just use the picture to get an idea. Then use your imagination to write an awesome story!

Glossary

dialogue: parts of the story where characters talk to each other.

event: something that happens in the story.

fictional: a story that did not really happen.

main character: the person that the story is about.

revised: took a second (or third!) look at your story to make your writing better.

sensory details: telling about how something in the story looks, sounds, feels, smells, and tastes.

setting: where and when the story takes place.

story map: a way to organize your ideas on paper to plan your story.

transitions: words and phrases used to move the story from one event to the next.

For More Information

Books

Dunn, Mary R. *I Want to Write Books*. New York: PowerKids Press, 2009.

Rau, Dana Meachen. *Ace Your Writing Assignment*. Berkeley Heights, NJ: Enslow Elementary, 2009.

Websites

Dot's Story Factory
http://pbskids.org/storyfactory/story.html

Write your story in the story factory and then add stickers, photos, or your own drawings.

Story Starters
http://www.scholastic.com/teachers/story-starters/

Choose a type of story and then spin the wheel to get fun ideas to help you start writing.

About the Author

Rachel Lynette has written more than 100 books for children of all ages as well as resource materials for teachers. She also maintains *Minds in Bloom*, a blog for teachers and parents.